. . . gun fhios.

agus a' feitheamh . . .

Chan eil fios agamsa gu dè
a th' ann . . .

ach tha mi a' dol a chumail
orm a' coimhead . . .

'S ann a tha mise toilichte gun do thagh rudeigin
fuireach san leas againne.

Tha an cù agam glè mhath air a bhith
a' cumail sùil air an toll.

Tha mi a' smaoineachadh gum bi e
ga fhaicinn na chadal.

Dh'inns mi dha Seanair is Seanmhair mun dràgon,
ach cha do chreid iad mi.

Tha Seanmhair ag ràdh gur dòcha gur e famh a th' ann.
Tha Seanair ag ràdh gur dòcha gur e broc a th' ann.

Ach tha mo dheagh
charaid ag ràdh gur
e dràgon a tha
a' fuireach ann.

Tha fios math aige,
oir tha dràgon a' fuireach
san leas aigesan.

Tha am beachdan fhèin acasan.

Sheall mi an toll dham charaidean.

no gun tig an t-acras air 's gun
tig e a-mach 's gun ith e mi.

Tha mo phiuthar ag ràdh gur dòcha
gu bheil beathach a' fuireach ann.

Tha i ag ràdh gum bu
chòir dhomh biadh
fhàgail aige . . .

Tha e dhen bheachd gu bheil
losgainn a' fuireach ann,
agus cha toigh leis losgainn.

Tha Dad ag ràdh an toll
fhàgail mar a tha e.

Tha Mam ag ràdh gur dòcha gur e doras a th' ann a-steach a thaigh luchag bheag.

Dh'fheuch mi rim bhàlla fhaighinn air ais
ach chan eil mo ghàirdeanan fada gu leòr.

Chan eil gàirdeanan Mam fada gu leòr
a bharrachd, agus chan fheuch Dad.

An uair sin shuidh mi gu math sàmhach . . .

agus chùm mi sùil airson deagh ghreis.

Chan eil fios agam gu dè a th' ann . . .

ach tha mi cinnteach gu bheil rudeigin shìos an siud.

Laigh mi air mo mhionach agus thug mi
sùil a-steach, ach chan fhaicinn dad.

Tha craobh san leas againne, agus tha toll beag faisg oirre.

Lorg sinn e aon latha nuair a bha mi a' cluich lem bhàlla.

Chaidh am bàlla dhan toll agus cha do thill e air ais.

Rudeigin

Rebecca Cobb

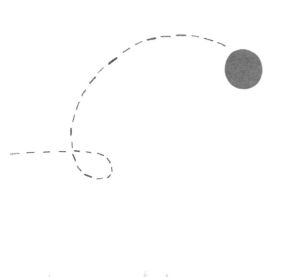

Do Richard

A' chiad fhoillseachadh sa Bheurla 2014 le Macmillan Children's Books,
An deasachadh seo 2015 le Macmillan Children's Books,
meur do Pan Macmillan, earrann de Macmillan Publishers Ltd,
20 Rathad New Wharf, Lunnainn N1 9RR Basingstoke agus Oxford
www.panmacmillan.com

1 3 5 7 9 8 6 4 2

A' chiad fhoillseachadh sa Ghàidhlig 2016 le Acair Earranta
An Tosgan, Rathad Shiophoirt, Steòrnabhagh, Eilean Leòdhais HS1 2SD

info@acairbooks.com   www.acairbooks.com

Tha Acair a' faighinn taic bho Bhòrd na Gàidhlig.

Fhuair Urras Leabhraichean na h-Alba taic airgid bho Bhòrd na Gàidhlig
le foillseachadh nan leabhraichean Gàidhlig *Bookbug*.

Gheibhear clàr catalog CIP airson an leabhair seo ann an Leabharlann Bhreatainn.

ISBN/LAGE 978-0-86152-417-4

Clò-bhuailte ann an Siona

THINGS WE USE

Plastic

RACHEL BLOUNT

TULIP
BOOKS®

Tulip Books Limited

© 2019 Tulip Books Limited

Tulip Books
Suite LP33738
20-22 Wenlock Road
London N1 7GU

Series designed by Jurian Wiese
Book designed by Keith Williams, sprout.uk.com

Production by Discovery Books

British Library Cataloguing in Publication Data
A full catalogue record for this book is available from the British Library

Picture Credits: Cover: Shutterstock: 3d_kot; Inside: Shutterstock: 3d_kot: p. 1; Alexey Androsov: p. 16; Big Foot Productions: p. 22br; Paolo Bona: p. 19; Rich Carey: pp. 21, 22bl; ESB Professional: p. 17b; FabrikaSimf: p 8; FamVeld: p. 14; Hasrullnizam: p. 4l; Hurst Photo: p. 20t; Iliart: p. 3; Dmitry Kalinovsky: p. 10l; Kittibowornphatnon: p. 18t; Pavel Kubarkov: p. 22t; Luliia Lysa: p. 17t; Milka-kotka: p. 10; Monkey Business Images: p. 13; Monticello: p. 4t; Sergey Novikov: p. 18b; Martin Christopher Parker: p. 20b; David Peterlin: p. 5t; Petroleum man: pp. 6-7; Alexander Raths: p. 12; S_Photo: p. 15; Sspopov: p. 9; TravnikovStudio: p. 5l; Trgrowth: p. 7t; Vldkont: p. 15t; Wavebreakmedia: p. 5b; Whiteaster: p. 5t; Wikimedia Commons: © Tomas Castelazo, www.tomascastelazo.com (http://www.tomascastelazo.com): p. 11; Fibermesh007: p 11l.

All the internet addresses (URLs) given in this book were valid at the time of going to press. However, due to the dynamic nature of the internet, some addresses may have changed, or sites may have changed or ceased to exist since publication. While the author and publisher regret any inconvenience this may cause readers, no responsibility for such changes can be accepted by either the author or the publisher.

ISBN 978-1-78388-145-1

Contents

What are plastics?   4

Where does plastic come from?   6

How is plastic made?   8

Moulding and shaping   10

Hard and soft plastics   12

Useful plastic   14

Plastics in our world   16

Plastic clothing   18

Recycling plastics   20

Plastics fact file   22

Glossary   23

Further information   24

Index   24

What are plastics?

Plastic is a very useful material. It can be turned into many different things. It is **waterproof** and can be made in lots of different colours. All of these things are made from plastic.

Truck

Toy bricks

Hoops

Skittles

Bottle

Plastic bag

Traffic cone

Ball

Most plastics are made from **chemicals** in factories. Plastics are also called **polymers**.

Snorkel

Goggles

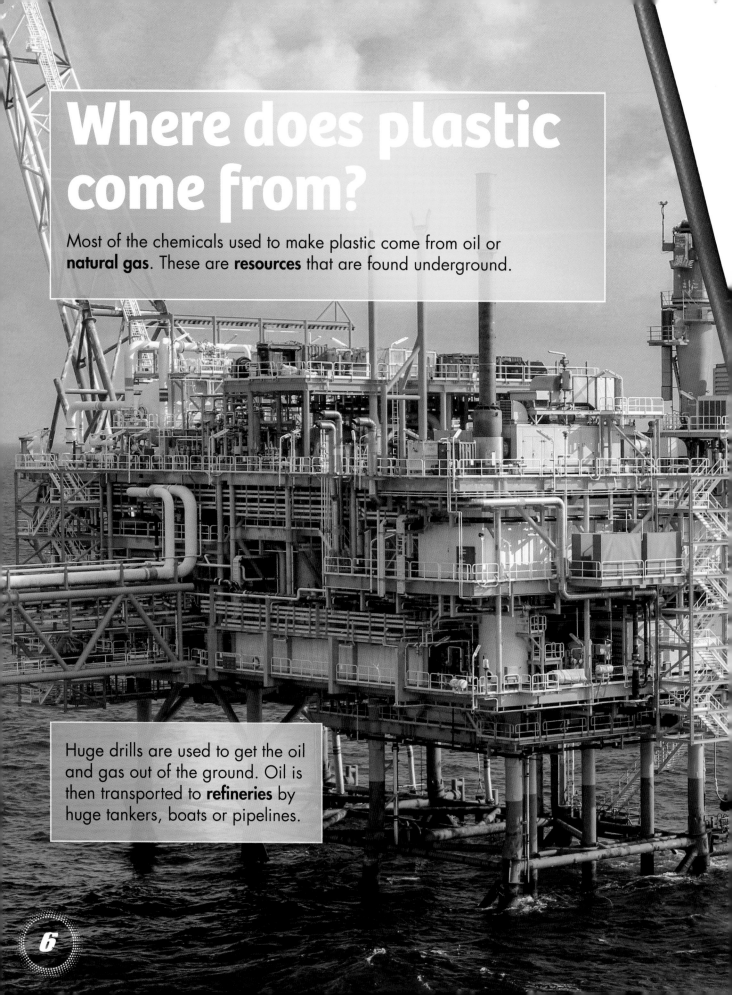

Where does plastic come from?

Most of the chemicals used to make plastic come from oil or **natural gas**. These are **resources** that are found underground.

Huge drills are used to get the oil and gas out of the ground. Oil is then transported to **refineries** by huge tankers, boats or pipelines.

Oil and gas resources

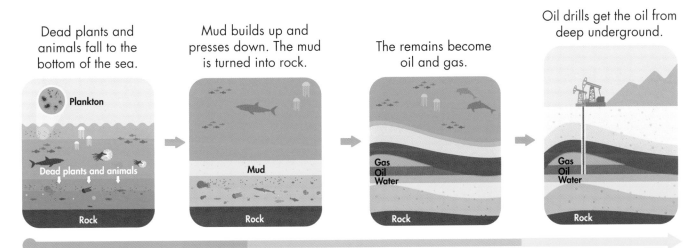

Dead plants and animals fall to the bottom of the sea.

Plankton

Dead plants and animals

Rock

Mud builds up and presses down. The mud is turned into rock.

Mud

Rock

The remains become oil and gas.

Gas
Oil
Water

Rock

Oil drills get the oil from deep underground.

Gas
Oil
Water

Rock

300 to 400 million years ago   50 to 100 million years ago   Present time

FAST FACT

Plants and animals that died millions of years ago were buried under layers of soil, mud and sand. Over time, they were turned into oil and gas.

How is plastic made?

Crude oil is processed at a refinery. Useful fuels, like diesel and petrol are taken out. Some of the chemicals left behind are used to make different types of plastic.

They are sent to a factory where they are first made into tiny plastic beads. Different **dyes** are added to make different coloured beads. These plastic beads are then reheated and made into lots of different things.

Sometimes, the plastic is made into sheets. These can be cut up and made into plastic bags.

Moulding and shaping

Some plastic objects are made using **moulds**. Plastic is heated until it is hot and runny, then it is poured into a mould. When the plastic **sets** it takes the shape of the mould.

FAST FACT

The word plastic comes from the Greek word *plastikos*, which means 'being able to be shaped and moulded'.

These giant plastic pipes were made in a huge mould.

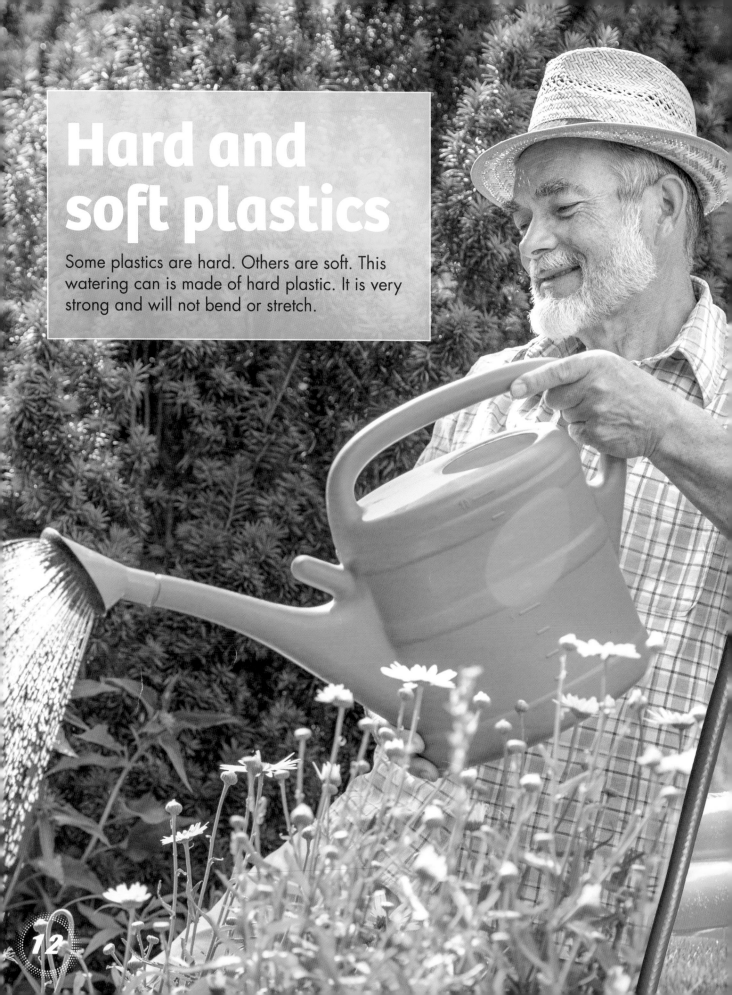

Hard and soft plastics

Some plastics are hard. Others are soft. This watering can is made of hard plastic. It is very strong and will not bend or stretch.

FAST FACT

One of the first plastics was made in 1907. Leo Hendrik Baekeland invented a hard plastic he called Bakelite.

This paddling pool is made of soft plastic. It stretches to hold water. The kitchen wrap used to protect our food is also made of a soft, stretchy plastic.

Useful plastic

Plastic is a very useful material. It is waterproof, and is used to make things like umbrellas that keep us dry.

These dangerous **electrical** wires are made safe with a plastic coating.

Plastic is also used to keep things warm. This plastic cup keeps the drink inside hot.

Plastics in our world

We use plastic things every day. Houses and buildings contain lots of things made of plastic, like these window frames.

Window frames

Many of our toys are made of plastic. Sports equipment is made from plastic too. Tennis racquets are made from plastic **fibres**.

Plastic clothing

Soft plastic can be made into long, thin fibres to make clothing. Scientists have invented lots of plastic fibres that are used to make clothes.

Many dressing up clothes are made from **polyester**, **lycra** and other plastic fibres, too.

These stretchy swimsuits are made using **nylon**, polyester and lycra.

Recycling plastics

Plastic doesn't **rot** away, so we must **recycle** it when we have finished using it. Plastic can be recycled and turned into new things, like benches or clothing.

WE RECYCLE

Recycled plastic bench

Plastic that is left lying around can harm animals and wildlife. It can get blown away and end up in our oceans.

Reduce the amount of plastic you use by shopping with reusable bags. Use metal straws for your milkshakes.

FAST FACT

A recycled fleece jumper can be made from 25 recycled plastic bottles.

Plastics fact file

Half of our plastic items are used just once and then thrown away.

It takes 500-1,000 years for plastic to **decompose**.

The Great Pacific **Garbage** Patch is a huge mass of plastic waste floating off the coast of California. It is three times the size of France!

Some supermarkets are banning single-use plastic in their stores.

Enough plastic is thrown away each year to circle the Earth four times.

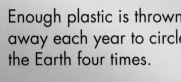
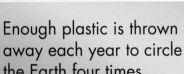

Glossary

chemical a substance that is often made in a science lab

crude oil a natural resource found deep underground

decompose to waste away

dye a chemical used to colour things

electrical to do with electricity; a source of energy that can flow through wires

fibres thin threads of natural or artificial material that can be used to make clothing

garbage rubbish

lycra an elastic man-made fibre used to make close-fitting clothing

mould container into which liquid is poured to create a shape when it hardens

natural gas a gas produced deep under the Earth

nylon strong, tough elastic fibres, used in textiles and plastics

polyester a large group of man-made fibres used to make textiles and many plastics

polymer another name for plastic

recycle to use things that have been used already; plastic, glass, paper and metal can all be recyled

refinery a place where something is cleaned or separated into different things; crude oil is processed into useful products

resource something that is found in nature and can be used by people

rot to waste away over time

set to go hard

waterproof able to stop water passing through

Further information

Books

Plastic (Materials), Harriet Brundle, Booklife Publishing, 2017

Plastic (Acorn: Exploring Materials), Abby Colich, Heinemann, 2013

Plastic (Materials), Cassie Mayer, 2008

Websites

Play a fun recycling game with Barnaby bear.
http://www.bbc.co.uk/schools/barnabybear/games/recycle.shtml

Explore this fun website with Tiki the penguin to find out all about plastic.
http://tiki.oneworld.org/plastic/plastic.html

Index

Baekeland, Leo Hendrik 13
Bakelite 13

chemicals 5, 6, 8
colouring plastic 8
crude oil 8

drilling 6, 7

Great Pacific Garbage Patch 22

hard plastics 12-13

lycra 18, 19

moulding plastic 10-11

natural gas 6, 7
nylon 19

oil 6, 7, 8

plastic coating 15
plastic fibres 17, 18
polyester 18, 19
polymers 5

recycling plastics 20-21

soft plastics 12-13, 18

useful plastic 4, 14-15

waterproof plastic 4, 14